**DOMINOES**

# Jemma's Jungle Adventure

*Anne Collins*

T0351767

Founder Editors: Bill Bowler and Sue Parminter

Illustrated by Cherie Zamazing

Anne Collins has written and adapted stories for readers of all ages. She has lived and worked in Greece, Turkey, Saudi Arabia, China, Qatar and Oman. As well as writing textbooks and Graded Readers, she works as a freelance journalist. She very much enjoys interviewing people, and believes that everyone has an interesting story to tell. She is passionate about wildlife conservation. She has also written *John F. Kennedy* for Oxford Bookworms Factfiles.

**OXFORD**
UNIVERSITY PRESS

# OXFORD
UNIVERSITY PRESS

Great Clarendon Street, Oxford, OX2 6DP, United Kingdom

Oxford University Press is a department of the University of Oxford.
It furthers the University's objective of excellence in research, scholarship,
and education by publishing worldwide. Oxford is a registered trade
mark of Oxford University Press in the UK and in certain other countries

© Oxford University Press 2015

The moral rights of the author have been asserted

First published in Dominoes 2015

2022

10 9 8 7

**No unauthorized photocopying**

Links to third party websites are provided by Oxford in good faith and
for information only. Oxford disclaims any responsibility for the materials
contained in any third party website referenced in this work

ISBN: 978 0 19 424565 4     Book
ISBN: 978 0 19 463962 0     Book and Audio Pack

Printed in China

This book is printed on paper from certified and well-managed sources

ACKNOWLEDGEMENTS

*The publisher would like to thank the following for their permission to reproduce photographs:*
123RF pp.iv (tropical frog/dirk ercken), 6 (Seychelles/Iakov Kalinin), 59 (green parrot/
kritsana piromrach), 59 (tiger/sattapapan tratong), 60 (beach in the Seychelles/Iakov
Kalinin); Alamy Images p.iv (bird of paradise/National Geographic Image Collection);
Getty Images pp.35 (Papua New Guinea/Reinhard Dirscherl), 57 (rainbow bee-eater/Julian
Kaesler), 59 (black rhinoceros/Tom Brakefield); Oxford University Press pp.iv (crocodile/
Nayong), iv (tiger in grass/Design Pics), iv (Eastern brown snake/Shutterstock), 59 (Asian
elephant/neijia); Shutterstock pp.iv (green chameleon/Fedor Selivanov), 56 (California
kingsnake/Eric Isselee), 59 (green sea turtle/Isabelle Kuehn), 59 (python snake/Ery Azmeer).
*Illustrations by:* Cherie Zamazing/The Bright Agency.

# Contents

**BEFORE READING**

**1** Match the pictures with the descriptions of the people. Use a dictionary to help you

**a** Yang Mie from China, expert on insects. ☐

**b** Richard Cave, expedition cameraman. ☐

**c** Dr Hamad Al Barwani from Oman, expert on snakes. ☐

**d** Dr Mark Malone from the US, expert on birds. ☐

**e** Ranu, one of the Madi people. ☐

**f** Jemma Parsons, an 18-year-old student. ☐

**2** Which of these animals do you think are in this story? Tick the boxes.

☐ crocodile  ☐ bird of paradise  ☐ tiger

☐ frog  ☐ chameleon  ☐ snake

# Chapter 1 – The golden feather

It was my last day at school. Mrs Green, my Science teacher, called me into her office.

'Come and look at this,' she said, **pointing** to her computer.

> ### Save The **Wildlife** (STW)
>
> ## STUDENT FOR **EXPEDITION**
> #### 1st August to 3rd September
>
> A group of **scientists** is looking for a student to help them on an expedition to the island of Kamora in the Western Pacific.
> Please email **Professor Yang Mie** at
> yangm@sww.uk.co

'I met Professor Yang Mie many years ago in China,' said Mrs Green. 'You're going to university in the autumn, Jemma. I know you want to make films about wildlife one day. If you're interested in this expedition, I'll write to her about you.'

'Kamora,' I thought. 'I've heard that name before. But where?' Then I remembered. When I was young, my grandfather told me about Kamora. I had something from Kamora too – something special.

**point** to show something with your finger

**wildlife** animals that live in a natural environment

**expedition** a difficult journey

**scientist** a person who studies the natural world

**professor** an important person who studies a lot and teaches

**Yang Mie** /yæŋ mjɛ/

Mrs Green sent an email to Professor Yang Mie, and three days later, I had a call from STW. They asked me to go to their London office the next day.

When I arrived, a woman showed me into a room. A man and a woman were sitting behind a table. The man was about forty, and well-dressed with short, dark hair. The woman was older than the man. She had a clever face with quick, bright eyes.

'Jemma Parsons?' said the woman. 'Please sit down. I'm Professor Yang Mie from **Shanghai University**.' She turned to the man. 'This is Dr Mark Malone from the University of California.'

I was very interested to meet Dr Malone. He was a famous scientist and an **expert** on birds.

'Well, Jemma,' said Professor Yang, smiling. 'Mrs Green's told us some good things about you.'

'Yes,' said Dr Malone. He was smiling too, but his smile was not very warm. 'But we want to ask you some questions. Why do you want to come on our expedition? You'll have to work hard and we can't pay you.'

'I'm not afraid of hard work,' I said. 'And money's not important for me. My **dream** is to make films about wildlife. There are many unusual animals and birds on islands like Kamora. I want to make films so that people all over the world can learn about them.'

'Yes, but a lot of other young people want to come with us,' said Dr Malone. 'Some of them have been on expeditions before. Why do you think you're better than they are?'

'Well,' I said. 'I've brought something special to show you.'

I took a large, golden **feather** out of my bag. The Professor and Dr Malone looked at it in surprise. 'That's a very interesting feather,' said Dr Malone slowly. 'Where did you get it?'

**Shanghai**
/ʃæŋ haɪ/

**university**
people study here after they finish school

**expert** a person who knows a lot about something

**dream**
something that you would like to happen; to see pictures in your head when you are sleeping

**feather** birds have these on their bodies to keep them warm and to help them to fly

'It's been in my family for many years,' I said.

'Can I see it?' he asked.

I gave Dr Malone the feather. He held it up and looked at it carefully. When the light **shone** on it, its colour was as bright as fire.

Dr Malone put the feather down on the table. His eyes were shining, and there was a strange look on his face.

'Can you tell us a little more about it?" asked Professor Yang.

'My grandfather was a sailor,' I said. 'He sailed to some of the islands in the Western Pacific. One of these islands was Kamora. One day my grandfather helped the **chief** of a village there, and the chief gave him this feather. He brought it home for my grandmother. She put it on her hat.

**shine** (*past* **shone**) to put light on something; the sun shines in the sky

**chief** the most important person in a group

3

'After my grandmother died, I found the hat inside an old box and I remembered my grandfather's story about Kamora. I looked carefully at the beautiful feather and I understood that it came from a very special bird. So I kept it in my cupboard and looked at it from time to time. Over the years, I began to have an important dream – to go to Kamora one day and find that bird.'

'Well,' said Dr Malone looking again at the feather. 'It's from a **bird of paradise**.' They're some of the most beautiful and exciting birds in the world. There are many different **kinds** of them, of course. But I've never seen a feather like this before.'

'Thank you for showing it to us, Jemma,' said Professor Yang, as I put the feather back into my bag. 'Now, do you want to ask us any questions?'

'Yes,' I said. 'Why are you going on this expedition?'

'Our expedition's the first scientific expedition to Kamora,' explained Professor Yang. 'There may be interesting new **species** there. Each of us is an expert on a different kind of wildlife. I'm an expert on **insects**, Dr Malone's our expert on birds, and we have an expert on **snakes** too – Dr Hamad Al Barwani from **Oman**. Perhaps you know something about his work?'

'Yes,' I said. 'Dr Al Barwani's done a lot of work on wildlife in the Middle East, and he's just written a new book.'

'That's right,' said Professor Yang smiling. 'You know a lot about the world of wildlife, I can see that. We also have a cameraman coming with us – a young man called Richard Cave.'

'It sounds very interesting,' I said. 'I'd love to come with you.'

'Yes,' said Dr Malone. 'But we're going to talk to other young people too.'

The Professor said she would call me the next day. But I was worried about Dr Malone. I felt sure that he did not want me on the expedition.

**bird of paradise** a type of colourful, beautiful bird

**kind** a type of thing; an apple is a kind of fruit

**species** (plural **species**) a group of animals or plants that are the same in some way

**insect** a small animal like a fly or a butterfly

**snake** a long thin animal with no legs

**Oman** /oʊˈmɑn/

Two days later, Professor Yang called me.

'Hello, Jemma,' she said. 'I've got good news for you. We'd like you to come to Kamora with us.'

'That's great,' I said. 'But what about Dr Malone? Are you sure that he wants me on the expedition?'

'Oh yes,' said the Professor. 'He wants you to help him find new species of birds.'

I could not sleep at all that night. I lay in bed and thought about the expedition. When I told my family and friends about the expedition, they were very excited too.

Then, one evening, I had a call from Dr Malone.

'I'm very pleased that you're coming with us, Jemma,' he said. 'There's just one thing. You know that feather of your grandmother's? Can I borrow it for a few days?'

'I'm sorry, Dr Malone.' I said. 'But I don't want to give the feather to anyone.'

'All right,' he said. 'It doesn't matter. But don't forget to bring it with you, will you?'

I was very busy for the next weeks, getting ready for the expedition. At last, it was time to leave. One month later, after a long journey, we arrived on Kamora by **helicopter**.

## READING CHECK

**Are these sentences True or False? Tick the boxes.**

|   |   | True | False |
|---|---|------|-------|
| **1** | Jemma makes films about wildlife. | ☐ | ☑ |
| **2** | Kamora is an island in the Eastern Pacific. | ☐ | ☐ |
| **3** | Professor Yang is from the University of California. | ☐ | ☐ |
| **4** | Dr Malone is an expert on birds. | ☐ | ☐ |
| **5** | Many young people want to go on the expedition. | ☐ | ☐ |
| **6** | Jemma's father brought a feather from Kamora. | ☐ | ☐ |
| **7** | There is more than one kind of bird of paradise. | ☐ | ☐ |
| **8** | Professor Yang wants to borrow Jemma's feather. | ☐ | ☐ |

## WORD WORK

**1 Find nine more words from Chapter 1 in the word square.**

| P | R | O | F | E | S | S | O | R | P |
|---|---|---|---|---|---|---|---|---|---|
| Y | H | B | E | K | T | C | Z | A | W |
| D | R | E | A | M | C | I | C | Q | I |
| J | V | W | T | E | F | E | H | I | L |
| R | S | N | H | O | L | N | I | N | D |
| E | X | P | E | R | T | T | E | S | L |
| D | G | U | R | X | B | I | F | E | I |
| S | P | E | C | I | E | S | Y | C | F |
| M | I | H | U | W | R | T | P | T | E |
| E | X | P | E | D | I | T | I | O | N |

**2 Use the words from Activity 1 to complete the sentences.**

**a** Jemma meets ..Professor.. Yang and Dr Malone in London.

**b** Jemma's ................. is to make films about birds and animals.

**c** The beautiful ................. is from a bird of paradise.

**d** The ................. of a village gave Jemma's grandfather a present.

**e** Professor Yang and Dr Malone are both .................s.

**f** Many young people are interested in the ................. to Kamora.

**g** Each scientist is an ................. in a different kind of ................. .

**h** Professor Yang knows many things about .................s.

**i** There may be interesting new ................. on Kamora.

## GUESS WHAT

**What happens in the next chapter? Tick four boxes.**

**1** The scientists start work on the island. ☐

**2** Dr Malone has a fight with a wild animal. ☐

**3** The Professor finds a new species of insect. ☐

**4** There is a terrible snowstorm. ☐

**5** Dr Hamad breaks Richard's camera. ☐

**6** Dr Malone is angry with Jemma. ☐

**7** Professor Yang climbs a mountain. ☐

**8** Jemma goes for a walk at night. ☐

# Chapter 2 – The camp on Kamora

**government** the people who control a country

**jungle** a hot place with lots of trees and wild animals

**camp** a place where people live in tents for a short time

**tent** a house made of cloth that you can take with you when you move

**lab** (*short for* **laboratory**) a room where a scientist works

**study** to learn about something

**release** to let a person or animal go free

**beetle** a small insect with a hard body and wings

Kamora was an island, in a group of islands with the same **government**. The largest island had towns and roads and an airport. But Kamora was smaller, with no roads at all. There were only rivers, hills, and lots of **jungle**.

Our **camp** was near a river in the jungle. Each of us had a **tent** for sleeping, and there was a large kitchen for all of us. Two men came to help with the cooking and washing. We had a **lab** too, where we **studied** the animals and birds we found.

The jungle was not an easy or comfortable place. At night it was so hot that it was difficult to sleep. I felt tired most of the time. Insects were a big problem too. Thousands of them came into the camp, looking for food.

My work was hard, but also interesting. There were so many new things to learn. I loved helping Professor Yang, and working with Dr Hamad Al Barwani, the expert on snakes. I liked Richard Cave too, the expedition cameraman. He was about twenty-five, with a friendly smile.

Every day we found birds, snakes, and insects. Some of these were new to science, and that was very exciting. We brought them back to the lab, and studied them. We took photos and wrote a lot of information about them. Then we took these living things back into the jungle and **released** them.

But sometimes there were problems between the different scientists. One afternoon, Professor Yang and I found a **beetle** under some leaves on the ground.

'I've never seen a beetle like this before,' said the Professor excitedly. 'I think it's a new species.'

**safe** in no danger
**disappear** to go away suddenly

The beetle was very unusual, with a large head and a gold and purple body. We took it back to the camp and showed it to the others. It was getting dark, so the Professor put the beetle in a box in the laboratory.

'It'll be **safe** here in the lab tonight,' she said. 'We'll study it in the morning.'

The next morning, the Professor was late for breakfast. When she arrived, she was looking very worried.

'What's happened to the beetle I found yesterday?' she asked.

'What do you mean?' said Dr Malone. 'Isn't it in the lab?'

'No, said the Professor. 'It's **disappeared** from its box. Look.' She held out the empty box.

'I saw you in the lab this morning, Richard,' said Dr Malone. 'Do you know anything about the beetle?'

'Well,' said Richard, slowly, 'I took it out of the box.'

'What!' said the Professor in surprise. 'Why did you do that?'

'I wanted to take some pictures of it,' said Richard. 'But after I finished, I put it back in the box.'

'But the top of the box was open,' said the Professor angrily.

'So you forgot to close the box,' said Dr Malone. 'And the beetle ran away. Well, perhaps it's somewhere in the camp.'

9

We looked everywhere for the beetle, but we could not find it. For the next few days, the Professor was angry with Richard.

One afternoon I was in trouble too. I was resting in my tent, when I heard Dr Malone calling me from the laboratory.

'Jemma! Come here! I need your help.'

I ran and found Dr Malone. He was holding a little bird in his hand. I could see its head and the top of its wings. It was bright red, yellow and blue.

'I found this bird in the jungle this morning,' said Dr Malone excitedly. 'Can you hold it for me while I take a photo? Sit down here, on this chair.'

I sat down and Dr Malone put the little bird into my hand. Its feathers felt soft and warm.

**spider** a small animal with eight legs that eats flies

**towards** nearer

Suddenly I looked down. I saw a large, hairy **spider** moving quickly across the ground **towards** my feet.

I screamed and jumped up from my chair. I forgot I was holding the little bird. I opened my hands and it flew out of the lab and high up into the trees.

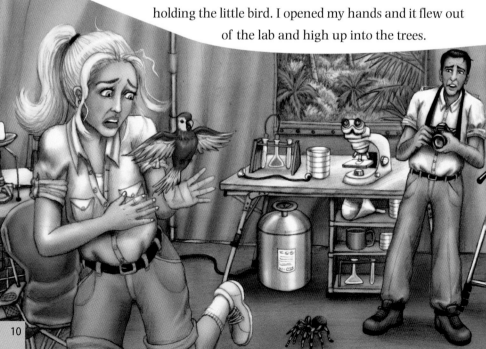

'You stupid girl!' cried Dr Malone. 'I'll never find that kind of bird again.'

'I'm sorry,' I said in a small voice. 'That spider gave me a terrible **shock**.'

'If you don't like spiders, why did you come on this expedition?' said Dr Malone. He walked away angrily. I felt very unhappy and I needed to talk to somebody. So later, I told Richard about the bird.

'Dr Malone will tell everyone what happened,' I said. 'Nobody will want me to work with them.'

'Don't worry, Jemma,' said Richard, kindly. 'It was just an accident. No one will **blame** you.'

'But Dr Malone blames me,' I thought to myself.

That night in my tent I could not sleep. I heard Dr Malone's voice in my head.

'You stupid girl... You stupid girl...'

I put my hand under my camp bed, where I kept the bag with my grandmother's feather. Yes, the bag was still there. It was good to know that it was safe.

'But I'll never find my bird of paradise,' I thought unhappily. 'It's just a stupid dream. Perhaps Dr Malone was right. I don't belong on this expedition. It's better for everyone if I leave.'

It was very hot and I felt thirsty. I got up and went outside to get a drink of water.

The trees were black against the night sky, but a bright moon shone down on the camp. I looked into the dark **forest**. Just then, I saw two eyes shining brightly in the trees. They looked like the eyes of a small animal. I moved nearer to the eyes but they disappeared. I started walking deeper into the forest.

Suddenly, I heard a voice behind me.

'Jemma! Don't move!'

**shock** a very bad surprise

**blame** to say that someone did something wrong

**forest** a place with lots of trees

## READING CHECK

**Correct the boxed words in these sentences.**

**1** There are `many` ....... no ....... roads on Kamora.

**2** Dr Hamad Al Barwani is an expert on `insects` ...................

**3** The beetle has a gold and purple `head` ...................

**4** Dr Malone sees `Jemma` ................... in the lab.

**5** The Professor is angry with `Dr Malone` ...................

**6** Jemma sees a `beetle` ................... moving across the floor.

**7** The bag with the feather is under Jemma's `table` ...................

**8** Jemma leaves her tent to get `a sandwich` ...................

## WORD WORK

**1 Complete the diary with the words in the box. Put the verbs in the correct form.**

| beetle | blame | camp | disappear |
|---|---|---|---|
| jungle | lab | safe | study | ~~tent~~ |

I'm sitting in my ...... tent ...... . It's very hot! Yesterday I
was walking with the Professor in the ................... when
she found a ................... . We brought it back to the
................... . But it was too dark to ...................
it. So the Professor put it inside a box, and took it to the
................... . She said it would be ...................
there. But now the beetle has ................... . We've looked
everywhere but we can't find it. The Professor ...................
Richard. She thinks he forgot to close the box.

**Match the words from Activity 1 on page 12 with the definitions.**

**a** ......lab...... a room where scientists work

**b** .................. not in danger

**c** .................. a place where people live in tents

**d** .................. to suddenly go away

**e** .................. a small animal with six legs

**f** .................. you can sleep outside in this

**g** .................. a place with lots of trees

**h** .................. to learn about something

**i** .................. to say that someone did something wrong

## GUESS WHAT

**What do you think happens in the next chapter? Tick the boxes.**

|  |  | Yes | No |
|---|---|---|---|
| **a** | Jemma decides to leave the expedition. | ☐ | ☐ |

| **b** | Dr Hamad catches a dangerous snake. | ☐ | ☐ |

| **c** | Dr Malone finds a bird of paradise. | ☐ | ☐ |

| **d** | Somebody steals Jemma's feather. | ☐ | ☐ |

# Chapter 3 – Up the river

I stopped. A few minutes later, Richard Cave came out of the trees. He shone a light on the ground. Something long and thin was pushing through the grass towards me – it was a snake. It moved nearer, and then rested at my feet.

'I'll go and get help,' said Richard quietly.

He went away and I waited. My mouth felt dry and my legs were shaking badly. At last Richard came back with Dr Hamad. Dr Hamad was carrying a long stick with a fork at the end.

'It's all right, Jemma,' said Dr Hamad quietly. 'Don't be afraid.'

He touched the snake's back with the stick, and it turned round angrily. It moved quickly, but Dr Hamad was quicker. He caught its head in the stick and closed his hand round its neck. I saw its small, black eyes looking up at me.

'This is a very dangerous kind of snake,' said Dr Hamad. 'You were lucky.'

'I saw you walking in the forest, Jemma,' said Richard. 'I hope you've learned your lesson. The jungle is a dangerous place. Please don't go walking by yourself at night again.'

The next morning, Professor Yang came and spoke to me.

'I've heard about some people who live up the river,' she said. 'They're called the Madi and they know many things about the wildlife on the island. I've sent a **message** to their chief, asking for his help. We'll go and visit them this afternoon.

'I'm going back to my tent now. I have to pay the men who come and help us. Can you tell the others that we're going up river, please, Jemma? Tell them to be ready by two o'clock.'

I quickly ran to my tent. I wanted to take the feather with me, so I took the bag out from under my bed. After that, I found Richard and Dr Hamad and gave them Professor Yang's message. They were very pleased about our plans to visit the Madi people. Then, I went to look for Dr Malone.

Dr Malone was in his tent. He was sitting at a small table with his back to me. I stood in the doorway and called his name, but he did not hear me. So I went inside the tent. To my surprise, there was a large **pile** of US dollars in front of him.

'Dr Malone...' I began.

Dr Malone turned round quickly. His face was dark and angry.

'What are you doing here?' he shouted. 'And what are you looking at?'

'I'm sorry,' I said. 'I called you, but you didn't hear me. The Professor asked me to give you a message. This afternoon we're going up river to the village of the Madi people.'

'Oh,' said Dr Malone. 'Oh, I see. Well, I'm sorry I shouted at you, Jemma. But you gave me a shock.' He saw me looking at the pile of dollars on the table. 'This money is for the men who come to help us', he said. 'Professor Yang asked me to pay them.'

'But the Professor's just paid them herself,' I said.

'Really?' said Dr Malone. 'Oh, I see.' He laughed. 'Well, I don't need to pay them then.'

**message** you write this to someone

**pile** a number of things, one on top of the other

'But why has Dr Malone brought all these dollars to the jungle?' I thought.

That afternoon we travelled up the river in two small boats. Professor Yang and Dr Malone were in one boat, and Richard, Dr Hamad and I were in the other.

The river was big and deep. On each side of the river, there were hills with forest. The trees of the forest came down to the **bank**. It was a beautiful day, and the water shone in the afternoon sun. Small insects danced on top of the water.

I put my hand into the river. The water felt cold and wonderful.

'Jemma!' shouted Dr Hamad. 'Don't do that! Look over there!'

I took my hand out quickly and looked. I saw something with a long body and **tail** disappearing into the water.

'The water's full of **crocodiles**,' said Dr Hamad. 'They'll **grab** you if they can, then pull you down to the bottom of the river.'

The day was hot, but suddenly I felt cold. The water still shone in the sunlight, but the river was not as beautiful to me as before.

After some time, we came to a high waterfall. Here, the water **poured** down the hill into the river and made a **whirlpool**. The water in the whirlpool was white, and turning round very fast. It looked very dangerous.

'Don't take your boat near there!' shouted Dr Malone. Richard made the **engine** of the boat go faster, and we drove quickly past the whirlpool.

**bank** the ground at the side of a lake or a river

**tail** the long thing at the back of an animal's body

**crocodile** this dangerous animal with short legs and a long tail lives in rivers

**grab** to take suddenly

**pour** water going from high to low

**whirlpool** water which is moving fast in a circle

**engine** the machine in a boat that makes it move

17

**hut** a little house

**land** the part of the Earth that is not the sea

**log** a long, round piece of wood, from a tree

At last, we saw some **huts** on the riverbank in front of us.

'That's the village of the Madi people, I think,' said Professor Yang.

As I looked at the **land** near the village, I was very surprised. The ground was empty of forest and there were large piles of **logs** standing by the river.

'That's strange,' I thought. 'What's happened to all the trees?'

A tall, young man was waiting for us on the riverbank.

'Good afternoon,' he said, smiling. 'My name is Ranu. Our chief is waiting for you. Please follow me.'

'Thank you, Ranu,' said Professor Yang.

As we followed Ranu through the village, the people came out of their huts and watched us. They wore clothes with bright colours, but they did not look very happy.

A young woman with a baby stopped Ranu and spoke to him. She looked at us with eyes that were full of hope. But when he spoke to her, she looked **sad**.

**sad** not happy

**translate** to change the language of something

'Was she asking about us?' said Professor Yang.

'Yes,' said Ranu. 'Her baby is ill and needs to see a doctor. But I told her you are all scientists.'

We came to a large hut and Ranu took us inside. A man was sitting on a carpet. He was no longer young, but he had a strong, clever face and quick, bright eyes.

'This is Chief Bhatta,' said Ranu. 'He doesn't speak English, but I can **translate** for you.'

19

## READING CHECK

**Put these sentences in the correct order. Number them 1–8.**

**a** The scientists start travelling up the river. ☐

**b** Ranu takes the scientists to Chief Bhatta. ☐

**c** Dr Hamad tells Jemma to be careful about crocodiles. ☐

**d** The Professor sends a message to the chief. ☐

**e** Jemma learns a lesson about the jungle. ☐1

**f** The scientists meet a tall, young man. ☐

**g** The scientists come to a dangerous whirlpool. ☐

**h** Dr Malone is angry with Jemma. ☐

## WORD WORK

**1 Find new words from Chapter 3 in the snake.**

**Complete these sentences with the words from Activity 1.**

**a** Professor Yang asks Jemma to give the others a .. message ...

**b** The young woman with the baby looks very ................. .

**c** There is a ................. on each side of the river.

**d** Jemma sees something with a long body and ................. .

**e** The ................. near the village has no trees.

**f** Dr Hamad tells Jemma there are .................s in the river.

**g** The water in the ................. is white.

**h** Jemma sees Dr Malone with a ................. of US dollars.

**i** A hungry crocodile can ................. a person.

## GUESS WHAT

**What happens in the next chapter?**

**a** Chief Bhatta *agrees / doesn't agree* to help the scientists.

**b** The scientists go *into the jungle / back to their camp*.

**c** Jemma shows Chief Bhatta *a picture of a bird / a golden feather*.

**d** The scientists eat a meal of *vegetables, fruit and fish / hamburgers and cola*.

**e** Jemma sees Dr Malone talking to a *beautiful girl / Ranu*.

**f** The Chief says that the village needs *a hotel / a school*.

**g** Richard carries *a pile of books / his camera* into the jungle.

**h** One of the scientists falls *into a small river / down a mountain*.

# Chapter 4 – Into the jungle

The Chief pointed to the ground and we sat down. A boy came in and gave each of us a drink. It tasted wonderful.

'Please tell Chief Bhatta that we've come to study the wildlife in the forest,' said Professor Yang. 'We'd like to ask for his help.'

Ranu translated, and the Chief replied in his language.

'The Chief is ready to help you,' said Ranu. 'But first he has something important to tell you.'

'We're a village of only a few hundred people,' said the Chief. 'Last year something terrible happened here. Many people became ill from **malaria**. But we had no money to buy **medicine**, so a lot of babies and young children died.'

'So that's why the people in the village looked sad,' I thought.

'Then some men from a **foreign company** came,' said the Chief. 'They asked us to sell them our land and trees. They said they would pay us a lot of money.

'We needed money for medicine. So I called a meeting of our most important people. We agreed to sell some of our land. Workmen came, cut down our trees, and made them into logs. Now they're taking the logs down the river to the sea.'

'Yes,' said the Professor. 'We saw piles of logs by the river.'

'Last week the men came back,' said the Chief. 'Now they want us to sell more of our land. I don't know what to do. If the men cut down our trees, they'll **destroy** our forest. Then the animals and birds will lose their homes and die.'

'I understand,' said the Professor. 'You love your forest and you don't want to destroy it. But you also have to think about your people. You have to do your best for them too.'

'Yes,' said the Chief. 'We need money for medicine, and we also need to build a school. You see, Ranu is the only person in our village who's been to school. We sent him away to study on

**malaria** an illness from mosquitoes

**medicine** something that you eat or drink to help you get better when you are ill

**foreign** not from your country

**company** a business

**destroy** to break every part of something

another island. That's where he learned English. But we need a school here – in our village.'

As I listened to Chief Bhatta's story, I began to feel very sad about the forest and the animals. I also felt worried about the people in the village, and their life in the years to come.

'You're scientists,' said the Chief. 'Perhaps you can find out important things about our forest, and help us to save it. We're ready to help you, but you must help us too.'

We were silent, thinking about the Chief's words. Then Dr Malone said, 'Show Chief Bhatta your feather, Jemma.'

I took my grandmother's feather out of my bag. The Chief and Ranu looked at it carefully.

'Have you ever seen a feather like this before?' asked Dr Malone.

'Yes,' said Ranu. 'It comes from a very unusual bird. But it doesn't live near our village any longer. You can only find it in one special place now, and that place is deep in the jungle.'

'Really?' said Dr Malone in an excited voice. 'Can you take us there?'

Ranu spoke to the Chief for a few minutes. 'Chief Bhatta says that tomorrow I can take you into the forest,' he said. 'But tonight, you must stay here with us.'

Ranu took us to some huts so that we could rest. That evening, the villagers gave us a wonderful meal with fish, and many kinds of vegetables and fruit. After the meal, a group of young men danced for us. On their heads, they wore feathers with wonderful colours.

I sat beside Richard, watching the dancers.

'Where did they get those beautiful feathers?' I asked him.

'From birds of paradise,' said Richard. 'Ranu told me that many years ago, the Madi people **hunted** the birds. They don't hunt them now, but they've kept the feathers for their dances.'

I was feeling tired so I said good night to Richard, and went back to my hut. On the way, I saw Dr Malone and Ranu standing under a tree. Dr Malone had his hand on Ranu's arm and was talking to him very fast.

'That's strange,' I thought. 'What are they talking about?'

Early next morning, I dressed quickly and put my grandmother's feather inside my **rucksack**. Then I went outside. The others

**hunt** to look for and kill animals

**rucksack** a big bag you carry on your back

were standing under the trees. They had their rucksacks on their backs and Richard was carrying his camera.

We followed Ranu into the jungle. It was a dark, strange world. The trees were so tall that you could not see the sun. But Ranu was an expert at finding his way. He moved quickly through the trees.

'The jungle all looks the same,' I said to Richard.

'Yes,' he replied. 'Sometimes people get lost in the jungle for days. They can't remember their way, and if nobody finds them, they die.'

**stream** a small
river

After three hours, I was hot and tired from carrying my heavy rucksack. Then we came to a **stream**. We all stood looking down at the water. It was moving very fast.

'I don't see a bridge,' said Dr Malone. 'How can we get across this stream?'

'Don't worry,' said Ranu. 'The water's not very deep. We can walk across.'

Ranu climbed down into the stream. At once, the water came halfway up his body. But he walked across easily, pushing against the strong **current**. Soon he **reached** the other side.

'It's all right,' he shouted. 'Don't be afraid!'

Next, Richard walked across, holding his camera high above his head.

Professor Yang climbed down into the stream and started to walk across. But then something terrible happened. She **slipped** and fell, and her head disappeared under the water.

**current** the way the water moves in a river

**reach** to arrive at a place

**slip** to fall suddenly

## READING CHECK

**Match the first and second parts of these sentences.**

| | | | |
|---|---|---|---|
| **a** | Many children and babies died | **1** | through the jungle. |
| **b** | Chief Bhatta agreed | **2** | the animals and birds will lose their home |
| **c** | Dr Malone asks Ranu | **3** | that the Professor slips and falls. |
| **d** | If the men cut down the forest | **4** | talking to Ranu under a tree. |
| **e** | A long time ago, the Madi people | **5** | because they had no medicine. |
| **f** | The current is so strong | **6** | where the bird of paradise lives. |
| **g** | Jemma sees Dr Malone | **7** | hunted birds of paradise. |
| **h** | The scientists follow Ranu | **8** | to sell the men some land. |

## WORD WORK

**1 Rearrange the letters in the logs to make words from Chapter 4.**

neecidmi

pyonmca

tdeosyr

maters

reuctnr

akkuccsr

nfeoirg

araalmi

**Use the words in the logs to make sentences about the story.**

**a** The scientists cannot get across the …stream… because there is no bridge.

**b** Jemma carries the feather in her ……………… .

**c** Some men from a foreign ……………… came to see Chief Bhatta.

**d** The Chief loves the forest and does not want to ……………… it.

**e** Last year, many people in the village died from ……………… .

**f** Chief Bhatta needs money to buy ……………… for his people.

**g** The ……………… in the stream is very strong.

**h** The company is from a ……………… country.

## GUESS WHAT

**What happens in the next chapter? Tick three boxes.**

**1** Jemma pulls the Professor out of the stream.  ☐

**2** The Professor is very ill with malaria.  ☐

**3** Jemma finds her bird of paradise.  ☐

**4** Ranu catches a bird of paradise, but it escapes.  ☐

**5** Dr Malone falls and breaks his leg.  ☐

**6** There is an unusual dance in the forest.  ☐

# Chapter 5 – A wonderful bird

I jumped into the stream. At once I felt the strong current around my legs, pulling me down. But I pushed against it and quickly reached the Professor. I grabbed her and held her head out of the water. Then I moved her towards the side of the stream.

Dr Hamad reached down and pulled the Professor out. He laid her on the ground in the warm sun. Her face was white and her eyes were closed. Dr Hamad looked at her carefully.

'She's all right,' he said. 'But she's had a bad shock.'

Richard and Ranu came back across the stream. We stood around the Professor, looking at her with worried faces.

After a few minutes the Professor opened her eyes. She tried to stand, but her legs were shaking.

'I'm so sorry,' she said. 'I don't feel very well. I don't think I can go on.'

'Don't worry, Professor,' said Dr Hamad. 'You'll be all right. We'll take you back to the village.' He turned to Ranu. 'Ranu, please go and bring help.'

After Ranu left, we moved the Professor out of the sun under a tree. I brought water from the stream for her to drink.

At last, Ranu came back with four young men. They were carrying a bed which was made of **rope**. They laid the bed on the grass and helped the Professor onto it.

'One of us must go back to the village with the Professor,' said Richard. 'She needs someone to stay with her.'

'I'll go,' I said at once.

'No, Jemma,' said Dr Hamad. 'You came here to find your bird. I'll go back with the Professor. We'll wait for you at the village.'

The men left, carrying the bed, and Dr Hamad walked beside them. Soon, they disappeared into the forest.

**rope** a very thick string

'Take us to the bird, Ranu,' said Dr Malone.

The three of us followed Ranu through the jungle. Sometimes he had to cut his way through the trees with a knife. I was afraid that snakes and spiders were hiding under the leaves.

The forest was noisy with the sound of birds, and sometimes we saw their bright colours in the trees.

At last, we reached an open place with trees all around.

'Sssh!' said Ranu. 'Don't make a noise. Look over there.'

I suddenly saw a very beautiful and unusual bird sitting on a **branch**. It was blue and red, with tall, green feathers on its head. The feathers in its tail were longer than its body. They were the colour of bright fire, just like my wonderful feather.

'That's it!' I said excitedly. 'That's my bird of paradise!'

Ranu moved silently towards the bird and we followed him. The bird watched us with bright eyes, but it didn't move.

'Why doesn't it fly away?' I asked. 'Isn't it afraid of us?'

'Perhaps it's never seen people before,' replied Richard. 'It doesn't know that people can hurt it.'

Just then, the bird made a strange noise. It jumped up to another branch and shook the feathers in its tail. Then it jumped again, turning this way and that way. It was dancing a strange and wonderful dance.

'Is it dancing for us?' I asked.

'No,' said Dr Malone. 'There's a **female** bird somewhere. The bird is dancing for her. Look, there she is!'

I saw a small, brown bird sitting on a branch. But I was not surprised. I knew that **male** and female birds of paradise look very different. Only the male birds have wonderful, bright feathers.

Dr Malone opened his rucksack and took out a **net** and a large **sack**. He gave the net to Ranu.

**branch** part of a tree

**female** a woman

**male** a man

**net** you catch things in this

**sack** a big bag

'Get ready to catch that bird, Ranu,' he said quietly. 'I want to take it back to the lab.'

The bird went on dancing for a long time. Richard took his camera and quietly began filming it. But suddenly the female bird flew away. The male bird stopped dancing and sat on the branch, looking after her.

'Quick!' cried Dr Malone. 'Now!'

Ranu jumped on the bird like a large cat, and threw the net over it. Dr Malone opened the sack and Ranu dropped the bird into it. Then he **tied** the sack at the top. The bird moved its wings and made a noise, but after a few minutes it was silent.

'Please don't hurt it!' I cried.

'Don't worry, Jemma,' said Dr Malone. 'Of course we're not going to hurt this wonderful bird. But we're scientists and our job is to study it. We can only do that in the lab.'

We went back through the forest and across the stream. At last we reached the village. Dr Hamad told us that Professor Yang was asleep in one of the huts. So we got into a boat and went down the river to our camp. Ranu came with us, carrying the sack. Dr Hamad stayed in the village with the Professor.

**tie** to keep something closed with rope

**cage** an open box to put animals in

Dr Malone went at once to the laboratory. He took the bird out of the sack and dropped it into a **cage**. The bird shook its bright feathers and sat in the cage, watching us. It still did not seem afraid.

That evening, as I was getting ready for bed in my tent, I heard voices. I looked outside. By the light of the moon, I saw Dr Malone and Ranu. They were talking together outside Dr Malone's tent, but I could not hear what they were saying.

'Why is Dr Malone always talking to Ranu?' I thought.

Next morning I worked with Dr Malone in the laboratory. We took photos of the bird, and wrote information about its body, head, wings and tail. I **admired** the quick way that Dr Malone worked. He really was an expert scientist. By lunchtime, everything was finished.

'Well done, Jemma,' said Dr Malone. 'You did a great job.'

'Thank you,' I said smiling. 'Are you going to take the bird back to the forest now?'

'Yes,' replied Dr Malone. 'Ranu will come with me. We'll release it in the same place that we found it.'

I felt sad that I would not see the wonderful bird again. But I was also happy that we were taking it back to its home in the forest. The forest was where it belonged.

'Can I come with you?' I asked Dr Malone.

'Of course,' said Dr Malone. 'I'll come and get you when we're ready to leave.'

I went to my tent for a rest. But I was tired from my morning's work and soon I was asleep. When I woke up, it was late afternoon.

'Oh no,' I thought. 'Why didn't Dr Malone call me?'

I ran to the laboratory, but nobody was there. The bird's cage stood empty and silent.

**admire** to think that somebody (or something) is very good

33

## READING CHECK

**Choose the correct words in these sentences.**

**a**  Jemma pulls the Professor out of a *whirlpool / stream / large river*.

**b**  Ranu comes back from the village with *three / four / eight* young men.

**c**  In the forest, Jemma is afraid of *crocodiles / wild animals / snakes and spiders*.

**d**  The bird of paradise is sitting on *a branch / the ground / the top of a tree*.

**e**  The male bird's feathers are all *blue and red / different colours / the colour of fire*.

**f**  Ranu catches the bird with *his hands / a large bag / a net*.

**g**  The bird's cage is in *the lab / Dr Malone's tent / Jemma's tent*.

**h**  Jemma and Dr Malone work together in the lab all *day / night / morning*.

## WORD WORK

**Use the words in the bird of paradise to complete the sentences on page 35.**

**a** The bed that the young men carry is made of ......rope...... .

**b** Jemma sees a beautiful bird sitting on a ................... .

**c** The ................. bird of paradise has very bright feathers.

**d** The ................. bird is small and brown.

**e** Ranu throws a ................. over the bird.

**f** Dr Malone opens a ................. and Ranu drops the bird inside.

**g** Ranu ................. the sack at the top.

**h** At the camp, Dr Malone puts the bird in a ................. .

## GUESS WHAT

**What happens to these people in the next chapter? Tick the boxes.**

### Richard and Jemma...

**a** ☐ follow Dr Malone up the river.

**b** ☐ have an accident in a boat.

**c** ☐ meet a dangerous animal.

### The Professor...

**a** ☐ leaves the island.

**b** ☐ finds an exciting new spider.

**c** ☐ learns what happened to her beetle.

### Dr Malone...

**a** ☐ takes the bird of paradise back to the forest.

**b** ☐ tries to steal the bird of paradise.

**c** ☐ falls down a hole.

# Chapter 6 – Secrets and lies

I stood looking sadly at the empty cage.

'What's the matter, Jemma?' said a voice behind me. I turned and saw Richard.

'I wanted to take the bird back to the forest with Dr Malone and Ranu,' I said. 'But they've gone without me.'

'Are you sure?' said Richard. 'Perhaps Dr Malone's still in his tent. Let's go and see.'

We went to Dr Malone's tent and called his name, but nobody replied. So we pushed back the doorway and went inside. There was a sweet, heavy smell in the tent.

'What's that strange smell?' I asked.

Richard picked up a small, empty bottle lying on a table and held it to his nose.

'Hmm,' he said. 'It smells like **chloroform**.'

'Chloroform!' I said in surprise. Suddenly I saw a small, golden feather on the ground. I picked it up and held it in my hand.

'You don't think that Dr Malone gave the bird chloroform, do you?' I asked.

'I don't know,' said Richard in a worried voice. 'But let's have a look around.'

I looked around the tent and saw Dr Malone's rucksack under the bed. I pulled it out and opened it. There was a small box inside. I opened the box and saw a large purple and gold beetle. I gave a sudden cry and closed the box quickly.

'That's Professor Yang's beetle!' said Richard. 'Malone blamed me for losing it, and the Professor was angry with me. But he took the beetle himself. We have to find out what's going on. Let's go to the village. Perhaps we can find Malone there.'

**chloroform** this makes animals sleep

We ran to the river, but only one boat was there.

'So Malone and Ranu have gone up the river,' said Richard.

'Come on, let's follow them.'

We jumped into the boat and Richard started the engine. He drove as fast as he could up the river. When we reached the village, we saw Dr Malone's boat on the riverbank. We pulled our boat up the riverbank too, then we ran to the huts.

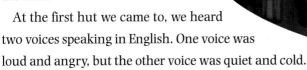

At the first hut we came to, we heard two voices speaking in English. One voice was loud and angry, but the other voice was quiet and cold.

'It's Dr Malone and Ranu,' I said.

'Sssh!' said Richard. 'Don't talk. They'll hear you.'

'Where's my money?' shouted Ranu. 'You **promised** to pay me today. I can't wait any longer.'

'Look,' said Dr Malone. 'I've told you. I can't take it with me while the others are still here. You'll have to hide it until they leave. I'll tell them I'm staying on the island to do more work. Then I'll come and get it, and I'll pay you the money. I've got it all ready in dollars, as we agreed.'

'All right,' said Ranu. 'But if you don't pay me, I'll kill it.'

I looked up at Richard, and said quietly, 'Are they talking about the bird?'

'Yes,' he replied. 'Come on! There's no time to lose.'

We ran around the hut and in through the doorway. Dr Malone and Ranu turned to us in surprise.

'What's going on?' asked Richard, looking around the hut. 'Where's the bird?'

'It isn't here,' said Dr Malone, smiling coldly. 'Ranu took it back to the forest.'

**promise** to say that you will certainly do something

'That's a **lie**!' I said. 'Ranu hasn't had time to do that. It's still here in this hut, isn't it?'

'I don't know what you're talking about,' said Dr Malone.

There was a pile of old leaves in the corner. I started to feel under the leaves. I pulled out a brown sack from the bottom of the pile. There was something big and heavy inside it.

'What's in here?' I asked. Then I started to open the sack.

'Give that to me!' shouted Dr Malone. He tried to grab the sack, but I pushed him away. I put my hand inside and pulled out the beautiful bird of paradise. Its eyes were closed and the long feathers in its tail **hung** down. It felt cold and heavy in my hands.

'What have you done to it?' I cried. 'Have you killed it?'

'You stupid girl,' said Dr Malone. 'The bird isn't dead. I gave it a little chloroform to **keep** it quiet.'

'But why did you give it chloroform?' asked Richard. 'You were taking it back to the forest.'

Suddenly I understood.

'But he wasn't taking it back to the forest,' I said slowly. 'He was stealing it. And Ranu was helping him.' I looked at Ranu. He was standing in a corner of the hut, silent and afraid. 'That's right, isn't it? Come on, Ranu, no more lies. Tell us what's going on. If you don't, I'll take you to Chief Bhatta.'

'No,' said Ranu. 'No, please don't do that.' He pointed to Dr Malone. 'I had to help him – there was no other way. He told me to say I took the bird back to the forest. He told me to keep it here secretly – in this hut.'

A **shadow** fell across the doorway of the hut. I turned and saw Professor Yang. Dr Hamad was standing behind her.

'I heard voices,' she said. She looked at each of us, then at the bird in my hand. 'Will somebody please tell me what's going on?'

**lie** not true

**hang** (*past* **hung**) to hold on at the top and go towards the ground

**keep** (*past* **kept**) to make something not change; to have somewhere

**shadow** a dark shape that the light makes behind or under things

'I'm sorry, Professor,' said Richard, 'but Dr Malone is a thief. He was stealing the bird of paradise.'

'And he took your beetle too,' I said.

The Professor looked at Dr Malone. 'Is this true, Mark?' she asked quietly.

Dr Malone did not reply. Suddenly, he pulled out a knife. Before I could stop him, he grabbed me. With one hand, he held my arms behind my back. With the other, he held the knife against my neck.

## READING CHECK

**1 What do these people say? Tick the boxes.**

*Jemma*

*Richard*

*Dr Malone*

*Ranu*

|  | | Jemma | Richard | Dr Malone | Ranu |
|---|---|---|---|---|---|
| **a** | 'I don't know what you're talking about.' | ☐ | ☐ | ☐ | ☐ |
| **b** | 'That's a lie!' | ☐ | ☐ | ☐ | ☐ |
| **c** | 'There's no time to lose.' | ☐ | ☐ | ☐ | ☐ |
| **d** | 'That's Professor Yang's beetle!' | ☐ | ☐ | ☐ | ☐ |
| **e** | 'Are they talking about the bird?' | ☐ | ☐ | ☐ | ☐ |
| **f** | 'But if you don't pay me, I'll kill it.' | ☐ | ☐ | ☐ | ☐ |
| **g** | 'The bird isn't dead.' | ☐ | ☐ | ☐ | ☐ |
| **h** | 'I had to help him – there was no other way.' | ☐ | ☐ | ☐ | ☐ |

**2 Are these sentences True or False? Tick the boxes.**

|  |  | True | False |
|---|---|---|---|
| **1** | The bird of paradise is in Dr Malone's tent. | ☐ | ☑ |
| **2** | Richard sees a small, empty bottle on the ground. | ☐ | ☐ |
| **3** | Jemma finds a box with a big spider inside. | ☐ | ☐ |
| **4** | There is only one boat on the riverbank. | ☐ | ☐ |
| **5** | Jemma hears Dr Malone shouting at Ranu. | ☐ | ☐ |
| **6** | Jemma says that Dr Malone is telling lies. | ☐ | ☐ |
| **7** | Dr Malone has not killed the bird of paradise. | ☐ | ☐ |
| **8** | Dr Malone holds a knife against Jemma's arm. | ☐ | ☐ |

## WORD WORK

**Use the new words in Chapter 6 to find the answers and complete the puzzle.**

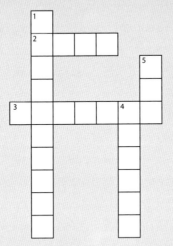

### Across

**2** the past of this is 'hung'

**3** say you will do something

### Down

**1** a chemical

**4** you see this when the sun shines

**5** something that is not true

## GUESS WHAT

**What does Dr Malone do in the next chapter? Tick one of the boxes.**

**a** ☐ He kills Jemma with a knife.

**b** ☐ He takes the bird back to its forest home.

**c** ☐ He escapes from the island by helicopter.

**d** ☐ He goes back to the camp.

# Chapter 7 – The chase on the river

The knife felt hard and cold against my neck. It was a terrible shock, and I dropped the bird. It lay on the ground at my feet. At once, Richard moved nearer to me.

'Stay where you are,' said Dr Malone, 'or I'll kill her.'

'Don't be a **fool**, ' said the Professor. 'Put the knife down.'

'Give me the bird first,' said Dr Malone. 'This girl is nothing to me. You decide, Professor. Which is more important? The girl or the bird? I'll give you ten seconds. One, two, three… '

'Stop!' said Professor Yang. 'All right, Mark, you win. Give him the bird, Richard.' Richard picked up the bird. He put it into the sack and gave it to Dr Malone. At once Dr Malone grabbed it. He pushed me away and I fell heavily to the ground.

'Good,' said Dr Malone. 'I'm leaving now. Don't try to follow me.' He pushed past us and disappeared through the doorway of the hut.

'Are you all right, Jemma?' asked Richard.

My arm hurt, but there was no time to think about that. 'Yes,' I said. 'I'm fine.'

'Come on!' cried Dr Hamad. 'Malone mustn't get away!'

'But what about the Professor?' I said.

'Don't worry about me,' said the Professor. 'Go after Malone. I'll take Ranu to Chief Bhatta.'

Richard, Dr Hamad and I ran out of the hut and down to the river. There were black clouds in the sky and it was beginning to rain. It was difficult to run quickly on the wet ground. Twice I slipped and nearly fell.

At last we reached the riverbank. Dr Malone was there, beside the boats.

**fool** a stupid person

Suddenly, he turned round. When he saw us, he took out his knife and held it up.

'I told you not to follow me!' he shouted. 'Don't come any nearer!'

We all stopped. Dr Malone threw the sack with the bird into one of the boats. Then he pushed the other boat far out into the river. At once the current began to carry it away. Then Dr Malone jumped into the boat with the sack, and started the engine. He drove away quickly without looking back.

'He's going back to the camp,' said Richard.

We stood watching our boat in the river. We were all thinking the same thing. How could we **chase** after Dr Malone now?

'Look!' said Dr Hamad. Suddenly, through the rain, we saw another boat out on the river. It looked like a small fishing boat. Our boat was moving towards it. There were two men in the fishing boat. One of them caught our boat. He tied it to the fishing boat with a rope. Then the men pulled our boat back to the riverbank.

We ran to meet the fishing boat. There were piles of fish in it. The two men jumped out, smiling. They cut the rope and pushed our boat towards us. We thanked the men, but there was no time to lose. We jumped into our boat and Richard started the engine. By now, it was raining very hard. We drove down the river, but we could not see Dr Malone's boat.

'I think we've lost him,' cried Dr Hamad above the noise of the engine. We came to a large **bend** in the river. As we drove around the bend, we saw something surprising.

**chase** to follow behind someone quickly

**bend** a corner

43

Dr Malone's boat was in the river in front of us. But it was not moving any more. It was at the place where the waterfall poured into the river and made a whirlpool. The boat was in the whirlpool, turning round and round in the dangerous, white water.

'Look!' said Dr Hamad. 'Malone's in trouble.'

Dr Malone was standing up in his boat, looking at the engine. He was trying to start it, but no sound came out. He tried again and again, but it was no good.

'My engine's broken!' he shouted. 'My boat's going to **sink**!'

'All right!' shouted Richard. 'We'll help you!'

Richard drove our boat slowly towards the whirlpool. But soon, we began to feel the whirlpool pulling us. Richard stopped the engine.

'I can't bring the boat any nearer,' he shouted. 'It's too dangerous.'

'Hurry up!' shouted Dr Malone. 'I'm sinking!'

There was a rope in the bottom of our boat. Dr Hamad took it and threw it to Dr Malone. It was difficult to throw the rope in the rain. He threw it again and again, but the rope was too short and it didn't reach Dr Malone's boat.

**sink** (*past* **sank**) when a boat goes down under the water

'It's no good,' shouted Richard. 'Jump into the water and swim to us!'

Dr Malone looked around. But his boat was sinking in the whirlpool. He grabbed the sack and jumped into the river, away from the whirlpool. His head disappeared under the water, but a few seconds later, we saw it again. He was a strong swimmer, but the current was stronger. It started to pull him away.

Richard drove our boat after Dr Malone. But suddenly Dr Hamad pointed to the riverbank.

'Crocodiles!' he shouted.

I saw three long crocodiles slip into the water. Dr Malone saw them too. He cried out and tried to swim to our boat. But he could not swim fast because he was still holding the sack with the bird.

'Drop the sack!' shouted Richard. 'Now, before it's too late.'

'I can't!' shouted Dr Malone. 'I'll lose the bird.'

'Don't be a fool!' cried Richard. 'Forget the bird. Do you want to die?'

Dr Malone still had the sack in his hand, but he could not hold it any longer. In the end, he dropped it and it sank down, down into the water. Then Dr Hamad threw the rope again and this time, Dr Malone grabbed it. He hung onto it with both hands.

We started pulling him towards our boat, but it was very difficult. His body turned this way and that way in the river, and sometimes his head disappeared under the water. But he still held on to the rope. I could not see the crocodiles, but I knew they were somewhere deep in the river.

At last we pulled Dr Malone to the boat. We grabbed him and tried to help him over the side. But his clothes were wet and heavy and it was difficult to hold him. He started to sink down into the water.

'Hurry!' cried Richard. 'The whirlpool's pulling us towards it.'

Suddenly Dr Malone screamed in **pain**.

**pain** the feeling that you have in your body when you are hurt

45

## READING CHECK

**Put these sentences in the correct order. Number them 1–8.**

**a** Dr Malone's boat is in a whirlpool. ☐

**b** Jemma and the others chase Dr Malone. ☐

**c** Dr Hamad throws a rope, and Dr Malone grabs it. ☐

**d** Dr Malone jumps into the river. ☐

**e** Richard gives the bird of paradise to Dr Malone. ☐ 1

**f** Jemma sees three crocodiles. ☐

**g** Dr Malone runs down to the river. ☐

**h** The sack sinks down into the water. ☐

## WORD WORK

**1 Find these new words from Chapter 7 in the crocodile.**

h s e a c

l o f o

n d b e

**Use the words in the crocodile to make sentences about the story.**

**a** The .................. on the river is very exciting.

**b** Richard drives the boat around a large ..... bend ..... .

**c** Dr Malone's boat begins to .................. .

**d** 'Don't be a ..................!' Richard shouts to Dr Malone.

**e** Dr Malone is in .................. .

## GUESS WHAT

**What happens in the next chapter? Tick the boxes.**

|  | Yes | No |
|---|---|---|
| **a** The crocodile eats Dr Malone. | ☐ | ☐ |
| **b** Jemma shoots the crocodile with a gun. | ☐ | ☐ |
| **c** The scientists go back to their countries. | ☐ | ☐ |
| **d** Dr Malone goes to prison. | ☐ | ☐ |
| **e** Richard makes some films about Kamora. | ☐ | ☐ |
| **f** A new expedition arrives on the island. | ☐ | ☐ |
| **g** Chief Bhatta and Ranu open a hotel. | ☐ | ☐ |

knsi

npia

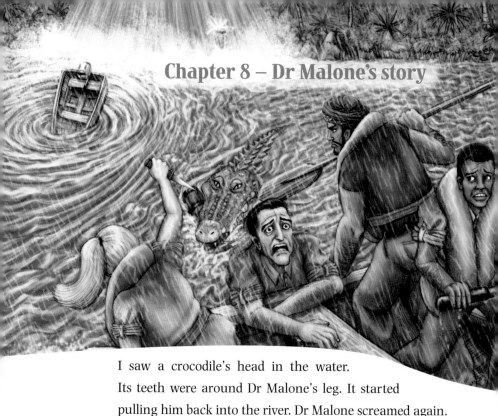

I saw a crocodile's head in the water.

Its teeth were around Dr Malone's leg. It started

pulling him back into the river. Dr Malone screamed again.

'Aaah! My leg!'

We began hitting the crocodile on the nose. But the crocodile still held on to Dr Malone's leg.

'My knife!' screamed Dr Malone. 'Get my knife! It's in my shirt pocket!'

I reached over and grabbed the knife from Dr Malone's pocket. My arm still hurt, but I took the knife and pushed it deep into the crocodile's nose. The crocodile opened its mouth in surprise and pain. It fell back into the water.

At once, Dr Hamad and I pulled Dr Malone into the boat. **Blood** poured from his leg, and ran onto the floor of the boat.

Richard took off his shirt and gave it to me. I tied it around Dr Malone's leg to stop the blood. Then we drove back to the village as fast as we could. Dr Malone's face was white and his body was shaking. He sat in the boat without saying anything.

**blood** this is red; you can see it when you cut your hand

It was good that he was safe, but I also felt very angry with him.

'Dr Malone is alive,' I thought. 'We saved him from a terrible death. But the bird of paradise is lost. It's at the bottom of the river. And it's all because of him.'

Professor Yang was waiting for us back at the village. When we told her what happened, she looked very unhappy.

'How could this happen?' she said. 'We came here to save wildlife, not to destroy it.'

Later, we took Dr Malone back to the camp. I put a strong **bandage** on his leg and gave him some medicine. He was still in pain, but after a time, the colour started to come back into his face.

Professor Yang called a helicopter to come and take Dr Malone to the hospital on another island. As we sat waiting for it to arrive, she said, 'Please explain something, Mark. You're a top scientist and a very clever man. Important people all over the world admire your work. It was a terrible crime to steal that bird. Why did you do it?'

'All right,' said Dr Malone. 'I'll tell you, if you really want to know.'

'It all started several years ago,' he said. 'I got a new job with the University of California, so I moved there with my wife. Rich people were living all around us, and I soon began to want a rich man's life too. I bought a big house and a fast car, and expensive clothes for my wife. Every year we went on wonderful holidays.

'But I didn't have the money for these things. I started to borrow money from the bank, but I couldn't pay it back. One day, I met a man at a party. I told him I was an expert on birds. He was very interested, and told me he was a **collector** of unusual wildlife. He asked me to bring him a **rare** bird from the jungle in Mexico. He said he would pay me $50,000.

**bandage** a long, thin cloth that you put on your body when you are hurt

**collector** a person who likes to buy and have lots of things of one kind

**rare** not usual

'At first I said no. But then one morning, I had a call from the bank. They said that they would take away my house and my car. So I went to Mexico and found the bird that the man wanted. I hid it in a special bag under my coat and **smuggled** it into the US. The man paid me $50,000. It was very easy money.

'A few months later, the man came to see me again. This time, he wanted a rare bird from a country in West Africa. I went there and got the bird, and smuggled it into the US. Again, he paid me well. After that, I brought him many different birds. Sometimes his friends wanted birds as presents for their children's birthdays. So I brought birds for them too. Sometimes I smuggled small animals and rare insects.'

'Yes,' I said. 'We found Professor Yang's beetle in your tent.'

'So you smuggle wildlife,' said Dr Hamad. 'You take animals and birds away from their homes in the forest and sell them for money.'

'Many of these birds and animals are very rare,' I said. 'And you're destroying them. Doesn't that worry you at all?'

'Yes, of course,' said Dr Malone. 'But a collector will pay a lot of money for a rare bird, you know.'

We were silent. We were all very shocked by Dr Malone's words.

'The helicopter will be here soon,' said Professor Yang. 'You will leave your computer here and you will not return to our expedition. Tomorrow I'll call the University of California and tell them what has happened. Do you have anything more to say?'

'Not really,' said Dr Malone. 'Only that I am sorry about the bird of paradise.'

That evening, I didn't sleep well. In the end, I got up and went outside my tent. Everything was very quiet. There was a beautiful moon, and hundreds of shining stars. I sat and thought about Dr Malone. How could his life have gone so wrong?

But most of all I thought about the bird of paradise. I remembered its wonderful feathers, and its dance in the forest. Now it could never dance again.

'Can't you sleep, Jemma?' said a voice.

I turned and saw Professor Yang standing behind me. 'Why couldn't I do more to save the bird of paradise?' I said sadly. 'Why couldn't I stop Dr Malone?'

The Professor sat down beside me.

'Don't feel bad, Jemma,' she said kindly. 'You couldn't save that bird. None of us could save it. But we can still do something. We can do our best to stop people smuggling wildlife for money, and selling birds and animals to rich collectors.'

I thought for a second and then said, 'You're right, Professor. Thank you.'

A few days later, we left Kamora. I looked out of the window of our helicopter. Its shadow moved over the trees like a strange kind of bird. I saw the island below us. I saw the blue sea, and the green jungle and the shining rivers.

'We found some new species on Kamora,' I thought, 'but we didn't learn everything about the island. It still has some secrets. One day I'll come back and find them.'

It's October and I've just started university. I'm in a different world now. The summer days have ended, and the trees in the park are losing their leaves. Kamora is like a dream. The golden sunshine and blue seas are very far away.

Professor Yang is writing a **report** about the new species of wildlife we found. She's going to send it to the government of the island group which Kamora belongs to. The report says that the forests and the wildlife are important to science. The Professor is going to ask the government to give the people of the islands more money, so they won't have to sell their land.

Professor Yang and Dr Hamad are very pleased with their work on the island. They found snakes and insects new to science. Richard is happy too. He made some wonderful films about the wildlife on Kamora and now a television company wants to buy them.

A few days ago, I read a story in the newspaper.

## TOP SCIENTIST *ARRESTED*

Dr Mark Malone, world expert on birds from the University of California, was arrested yesterday at his home for the crime of smuggling rare birds into the United States.

I still have my grandmother's feather. I've made a promise to myself and the lost bird. Well, two promises. The first is that one day I'll go back to Kamora. The second is that I'll do everything I can to save the wildlife on Kamora and in other places too.

**report** what someone writes to explain something

**arrest** when the police take someone to prison

I learned many things from the expedition. I learned about the work of scientists, and I learned about new kinds of wildlife. I also learned about the dark side of life, and that sometimes people can lose their way.

I'll never forget the bird of paradise. It's given me hope. You think you can do nothing, but you can always do something. One day my films will help to save the lives of rare and wonderful birds and animals. I'm very sure about that.

# ACTIVITIES

## READING CHECK

**Find the correct words in Professor Yang's email to the University of California.**

**To:** University of California
**From:** Professor Yang

I am writing to you about Dr Mark Malone, the world famous expert on **(a)** *snakes / (birds)* who works for your **(b)** *company / university*.

We are a group of **(c)** *scientists / students* who are on **(d)** *an expedition / a holiday* on the island of Kamora. I am sorry to tell you that Dr Malone has **(e)** *escaped from / left* our expedition. I had to **(f)** *send / chase* him away. He gave a man from a **(g)** *village / town* here a lot of money to **(h)** *steal / buy* a rare **(i)** *bird / animal*.

I am very **(j)** *sorry / happy* to write with this **(k)** *bad / good* news about Dr Malone. He has been a **(l)** *gold / wildlife* smuggler for a long time. He has made a lot of money from selling **(m)** *rare / dangerous* birds and animals to rich **(n)** *smugglers / collectors*.

I have told Dr Malone that he cannot return to our **(o)** *expedition / adventure*.

Yang Mie

## WORD WORK

**1 Find the new words from Chapter 8 in the whirlpool.**

**Match the words from Activity 1 with the definitions.**

**a** ....blood.... it is red, and in your body
**b** ................ the police do this if they think you are a thief
**c** ................ very unusual
**d** ................ a person who collects things
**e** ................ you may need this if you cut yourself
**f** ................ Professor Yang writes this
**g** ................ it is a terrible crime to do this to wildlife

## GUESS WHAT

**It is a year after the story ends. What has happened to these people? Tick the boxes. There might be more than one box for each sentence. Then think of some ideas of your own.**

*Jemma*    *Richard*    *Dr Malone*    *Professor Yang*    *Dr Hamad*

| | Jemma | Richard | Dr Malone | Prof Yang | Dr Hamad |
|---|---|---|---|---|---|
| **a** planning a new expedition | ☐ | ☐ | ☐ | ☐ | ☐ |
| **b** often on TV | ☐ | ☐ | ☐ | ☐ | ☐ |
| **c** at university in London | ☐ | ☐ | ☐ | ☐ | ☐ |
| **d** in prison in the US | ☐ | ☐ | ☐ | ☐ | ☐ |
| **e** writing a book about snakes | ☐ | ☐ | ☐ | ☐ | ☐ |
| **f** wants to go back to Kamora | ☐ | ☐ | ☐ | ☐ | ☐ |
| **g** is happy with life | ☐ | ☐ | ☐ | ☐ | ☐ |
| **h** ............................ | ☐ | ☐ | ☐ | ☐ | ☐ |
| **i** ............................ | ☐ | ☐ | ☐ | ☐ | ☐ |

## Project A  *Writing about an animal*

**1** **Read the notes that Dr Hamad wrote about a new species of snake he found. Fill in his notes with the missing words in the box.**

| birds   hunts   leaves   thin   trees   white |
| --- |

| Species | snake |
| --- | --- |
| How long | 2 metres |
| Colours | black and ................ |
| What it looks like | long, ................ body, small head |
| When and where we found it | 16th July, early morning, under some ................ |
| What it eats | small ................ and animals |
| Where it lives | in ................, on the ground |
| Other information | ................ at night |

**2** **Correct the mistakes in Dr Hamad's report.**

On 17th July, late at night, we found a new species of bird. It was 3 metres long and was black and yellow. It had a long, thin body and a large head. It lives in rivers and on the ground. It eats small insects and animals. It hunts in the day.

Imagine that you found this bird. Fill in the information in the table about it.

| Species | |
|---|---|
| How long – tail, wings, legs, head | |
| Colours | |
| What it looks like (feathers) | |
| When and where we found it | |
| What it eats | |
| Where it lives | |
| Other information | |

Use your notes to write a report about the bird.

Choose an interesting or unusual animal or bird from your country. Write some notes about it, then write a report.

## Project B *Stop crime against wildlife!*

**1** **Professor Yang is on TV, talking about the expedition to Kamora. Choose the best question word for each question. Then match Professor Yang's answers to the questions.**

| How | How long | How many | What | When | Where | ~~Who~~ | Why |
|---|---|---|---|---|---|---|---|

**1** ......Who...... went with you on the expedition?

**2** .................. did you decide to go to Kamora?

**3** .................. was your camp?

**4** .................. did you stay on Kamora?

**5** .................. new species did you find?

**6** .................. is your next expedition?

**7** .................. was the weather like on Kamora?

**8** .................. did you travel to Kamora?

**a** Near a river in the jungle

**b** About a month

**c** By helicopter

**d** Maybe next year

**e** We were hoping to find some new species there.

**f** Dr Malone, Dr Hamad Al Barwani, Richard Cave and Jemma Parsons

**g** More than twenty different kinds

**h** Very hot

**2** **Professor Yang is answering questions about wildlife smuggling. Put these words in the right order to make questions.**

**1** *people / do / wildlife / smuggle / Why?* ..................................................

**2** *does / In / countries / what / it / happen?* ..................................................

**3** *governments / this / can / crime / How / stop?* ..................................................

**4** *most / danger / animals / What / in / are?* ..................................................

**5** *do / What / help / can / we / to?* ..................................................

**Choose one of these animals. They are all in danger from wildlife smugglers.**

**Find out as much as you can about this animal and write some notes. Think about:**

- what it looks like
- what countries it lives in
- what kind of place it lives in (for example, the jungle, or the sea)
- why people smuggle it (or part of it)
- what people or governments are doing to stop this
- what you can do to help stop this

**4** **Find another student with a different animal. Write five things you would like to know about the other student's animal.**

1 .... How many of these animals are there in the world?

2 .................................................................................

3 .................................................................................

4 .................................................................................

5 .................................................................................

**Imagine that you are on television, as an expert on your animal.**

**Student A:**  Give a talk about your animal.

**Student B:**  Ask Student A questions about their animal.

**5** **Work with two or three other students. Think of an environmental problem. Learn a[s] much as possible about the problem. Then tell the class about it. Say:**

- ◆ what the problem is
- ◆ why you are worried about it
- ◆ how the problem began
- ◆ what is happening to stop it
- ◆ what you can do to help

## GRAMMAR CHECK

### Present Perfect and Past Simple

We use the Present Perfect for:

– things that happened at an indefinite time in the past (we can use just when this time is very recent)

*Jemma has just started university.*

– experiences in our lives (we can use never to mean at no time)

*Most young people have never been on a scientific expedition.*

*Richard has made a lot of films.*

– things that started in the past and continue up to the present

*The Madi people have lived on Kamora for a long time.*

We use the Past Simple for finished past events.

*Dr Malone jumped into the boat and drove quickly up the river.*

**1** **Jemma and Richard meet for coffee in London. Complete their conversation with the words and verbs in brackets. Use the Present Perfect or Past Simple.**

**Richard:** Hi, Jemma, good to see you. How are you?

**Jemma:** Fine, thanks. I **a)** ...'ve been... at university for two weeks now. How's everything with you?

**Richard:** Great. Last Tuesday I **b)** ................. (have) a meeting with a TV company. I **c)** ................. (show) them my film about Kamora. They really **d)** ................. (like) it.

**Jemma:** Wow! How exciting. Oh, I **e)** ................. (sent) Professor Yang an email last week, but I **f)** ................. (not had) any reply. But I **g)** ................. (hear) from Dr Hamad yesterday. He **h)** ................. (finish) his new book.

**Richard:** Yes, I know. It's called *Snakes of the Middle East*. And he **i)** ................. (invite) me to Oman next year. He **j)** ................. (ask) me to make a film about the wildlife there.

**Jemma:** What about Dr Malone?

**Richard:** Well, I **k)** ................. (read) something about him in the newspaper last week.

**Jemma:** Yes, I **l)** ................. (see) that story too. But there **m)** ................. (not be) any more news since then.

## GRAMMAR CHECK

### Comparative adjectives

We use a comparative adjective + than to say that two people or things are different in some way.

*Dr Malone is older than Richard Cave.*

| To make comparative adjectives, we add -er to most short adjectives. | *young – younger* |
|---|---|
| When adjectives finish in -e, we add -r. | *safe – safer* |
| When adjectives finish in a consonant + y, we change the y to i and add -er. | *easy – easier* |
| When adjectives finish in a short vowel + consonant, we double the consonant and add -er. | *hot – hotter* |
| With adjectives of three syllables or more, we put more before the adjective. | *difficult – more difficult* |

## 2 Complete the sentences. Use the comparative form of the adjectives in brackets.

**a** Kamora is ...smaller... (small) than many of the other islands in the group.

**b** The jungle is ................. (dangerous) at night than by day.

**c** The ground near the river is ................. (wet) than the ground near the tents.

**d** Dr Malone's tent is ................. (comfortable) than Jemma's.

**e** The current near the whirlpool is ................. (strong) than near the riverbank.

**f** The river is much ................. (deep) and ................. (wide) than the stream.

**g** The male bird of paradise is ................. (beautiful) than the female.

**h** Jemma's rucksack is ................. (heavy) than Richard's.

**i** Chief Bhatta's hut is ................. (large) than the other huts in the village.

**j** Ranu is ................. (tall) than Professor Yang.

**k** Jemma's bird of paradise is ................. (rare) than some other kinds.

## GRAMMAR CHECK

### Question tags

We use question tags to check information, or to ask someone to agree.

*Kamora's an island in the Western Pacific Ocean, isn't it?*

The tag contains subject + main verb or auxiliary verb to match the sentence.

*Jemma went on the expedition too, didn't she?*

*Birds of paradise are rare, aren't they?*

When the sentence is affirmative, the tag is negative.

*You want to make films about wildlife, don't you?*

When the sentence is negative, the tag is affirmative.

*You haven't seen my beetle, have you?*

**3 Complete the sentences with the question tags in the box.**

| | | | | |
|---|---|---|---|---|
| didn't he | aren't they | isn't it | do they | has she |
| doesn't it | ~~don't they~~ | does he | | |

a The scientists arrive on Kamora by helicopter, ..*don't they*..?

b Professor Yang's beetle disappears, .....................?

c Dr Hamad doesn't kill the snake, .....................?

d The Madi people don't have money to buy medicine, .....................?

e Birds of paradise are wonderful, .....................?

f Jemma hasn't been on an expedition before, .....................?

g Jemma's grandfather visited Kamora a long time ago, .....................?

h Wildlife smuggling is a terrible crime, .....................?

**4 Complete the sentences about these people with question tags.**

a Dr Malone is an expert on birds, ...*isn't he*....?

b Richard makes films about wildlife, .....................?

c Dr Hamad isn't from Saudi Arabia, .....................?

d Chief Bhatta doesn't want to sell land, .....................?

e Ranu can speak English well, .....................?

f Jemma and Richard haven't met before, .....................?

## GRAMMAR CHECK

### Direct and reported speech

| In direct speech, we give the words that people say or think. | In reported speech, we put the verb one step into the past and change the pronouns and possessive adjectives. |
|---|---|
| *'Your feather is from a bird of paradise,' said Dr Malone.* | *Dr Malone said that my feather was from a bird of paradise.* |
| *'I'll go and get help,' said Richard.* | *Richard said that he would go and get help.* |

We change personal pronouns and possessive adjectives in reported speech to match the speaker and the situation, too.

**5** **Rewrite these direct speech sentences as reported speech.**

**a** 'I've got good news for you,' said Professor Yang.
.....Professor Yang said that she had good news for me.....

**b** 'The water's full of crocodiles,' said Dr Hamad.
.......................................................................................

**c** 'I don't know what to do,' said Chief Bhatta.
.......................................................................................

**d** 'We can walk across the stream,' said Ranu.
.......................................................................................

**e** 'I don't think I can go on,' said Professor Yang.
.......................................................................................

**f** 'I'll go back with the Professor,' said Dr Hamad.
.......................................................................................

**g** 'It smells like chloroform,' said Richard.
.......................................................................................

**h** 'I can't wait any longer,' said Ranu.
.......................................................................................

**i** 'I'm leaving now,' said Dr Malone.
.......................................................................................

**j** 'I'll take Ranu to Chief Bhatta,' said Professor Yang.
.......................................................................................

## GRAMMAR CHECK

### *Going to* future: affirmative and negative

We make going to future affirmative with the verb am / is / are + going to + infinitive.

*Men from foreign companies are going to come to Kamora and cut down the trees.*

We make going to future negative with am not / isn't / aren't + going to + infinitive.

*'We're not going to hurt this wonderful bird of paradise,' said Dr Malone.*

We can use going to future to talk about intentions.

*'Are you going to take the bird back to the forest?' I asked.*

We can also use going to future to make predictions.

*'My engine's broken!' he shouted. 'My boat's going to sink!'*

**6** **Complete the sentences. Use the affirmative or negative form of *going to* and the verbs in brackets.**

**a** Professor Yang and Dr Malone ...*are going to talk*... (talk) to many young people.

**b** The scientists ................................... (not travel) to Kamora by ship.

**c** They ................................... (not stay) in a hotel.

**d** They ................................... (look) for new species of wildlife.

**e** 'Come on! We're ................................... (follow) Dr Malone!' said Dr Hamad.

**f** Professor Yang ................................... (write) a report about the expedition.

**g** Jemma ................................... (not forget) the bird of paradise.

**7** **Use these words to make sentences. Use the affirmative or negative form of *going to*.**

**a** Professor Yang / plan / new expedition.

....*Professor Yang is going to plan a new expedition.*...........

**b** Dr Hamad / not leave / Oman for some time.

...................................................................................... .

**c** The government of the islands / give / some money / Chief Bhatta.

...................................................................................... .

**d** Dr Malone / never go back / Kamora.

...................................................................................... .

**e** Jemma / be / famous / filmmaker / one day.

...................................................................................... .

## GRAMMAR CHECK

**Time clauses with *before*, *after*, *when*, and *while***

Before links a later action with an earlier action.

*Before the scientists went into the jungle, they stayed for a night in the village.*

After links an earlier action with a later action.

*After the Professor caught the beetle, she put it in a box in the lab.*

When links two actions close in time, often where the first action is the reason for the second action.

*When Dr Malone saw Jemma's feather, he became very interested in it.*

While is used for two actions happening at the same time, or for a background action that is going on when something else happens.

*While the scientists were travelling up the river, they saw some crocodiles.*

We can put before, after, when, and while clauses at the end of the sentence.

*Jemma had a lot of things to get ready before she went on the expedition.*

**8  Complete this page from Jemma's diary with *before*, *after*, *when* or *while*.**

Today was a very exciting day. **a)** .....After..... we left the village, Ranu took us into the jungle. We came to a small stream, but **b)** ................. Professor Yang was walking across, she slipped and fell. We pulled her out of the water, but **c)** ................. we saw that she did not look well, Dr Hamad sent Ranu back to the village for help. **d)** ................. we were waiting for Ranu to return, I looked after the Professor. **e)** ................. Ranu came back, he had four strong young men with him. They put the Professor on a bed made of rope. **f)** ................. they left, Dr Hamad said he would go back to the village with them.

**g)** ................. the men left, Richard, Dr Malone and I followed Ranu through the jungle. **h)** ................. we were walking, we heard the sound of many birds, but we could not see them. Suddenly, we saw a beautiful male bird of paradise. **i)** ................. I saw this bird, I felt very excited. It was the bird I was looking for! The bird started to dance. Then we saw that **j)** ................. the bird was dancing, a female bird was watching it. **k)** ................. the male bird stopped dancing, the female bird flew away. So Ranu threw a net over the male bird **l)** ................. he could fly away too. **m)** ................. Ranu caught the bird, he dropped it into a sack.

## GRAMMAR CHECK

### Prepositions of place

We use prepositions of place to say where things are.

over •     behind ▢▸     between ▢•▢     in ▢•

in front of ▢•     near ▢ •     under •     on •

### Complete the sentences using prepositions.

**a** Dr Malone had a large pile of US dollars ...in front of........ him.

**b** The helicopter's shadow moved ............................. the trees.

**c** The bird of paradise was sitting ............................. a branch in the forest.

**d** Jemma keeps the feather ............................. her bed.

**e** The land ............................. the river was empty of forest.

**f** Professor Yang and Dr Malone were sitting ............................. a table.

**g** There are some dangerous snakes ............................. the jungle.

**h** The lab is ............................. Dr Malone's tent and Professor Yang's tent.

### Choose the correct preposition in each of these sentences.

**a** Jemma saw a small golden feather *in / on / over* the ground.

**b** The village of the Madi people was *in / behind / near* the river.

**c** Dr Malone held Jemma's arms *in front of / behind / above* her back.

**d** Jemma saw Dr Malone and Ranu talking *under / over / in* a tree.

**e** Ranu threw the net *in front of / between / over* the bird of paradise.

**f** The whirlpool was *on / in / under* the river.

**g** The camp was *between / in / on* the river and the jungle.

**h** Richard and Jemma saw Dr Malone's boat *on / under / in front of* them.

# DOMINOES Your Choice

Read *Dominoes* for pleasure, or to develop language skills. It's your choice.

Each *Domino* reader includes:
- a good story to enjoy
- integrated activities to develop reading skills and increase vocabulary
- task-based projects – perfect for CEFR portfolios
- contextualized grammar activities

Each *Domino* pack contains a reader, and an excitingly dramatized audio recording of the story

If you liked this *Domino*, read these:

### Green Planet
*Christine Lindop*

Once 'green' was just a colour. Now we use it to talk about a way of looking at our world and thinking about the environment. But how green is our planet today?

From nuclear power plants to Nemo the clownfish, from polar bears to pesticides, from Greenpeace to global warming, this book brings together many different stories that have made environmental history.

Read it, and perhaps you too can help to make our planet greener!

### The Lost World
*Sir Arthur Conan Doyle*

'You said that you wanted danger, didn't you?' says McArdle, the editor of the Daily Gazette. And he sends his young reporter, Malone, on a strange journey into South America with the famous Professor Challenger.

Challenger believes that he can find a lost world full of dinosaurs in the middle of the Amazon Forest. But this world is dangerous to reach, and, once the Professor and his small group of explorers arrive, things get even more dangerous for them.

Will they return alive?

|  | CEFR | Cambridge Exams | IELTS | TOEFL iBT | TOEIC |
|---|---|---|---|---|---|
| Level 3 | B1 | PET | 4.0 | 57-86 | 550 |
| Level 2 | A2–B1 | KET-PET | 3.0-4.0 | – | 390 |
| Level 1 | A1–A2 | YLE Flyers/KET | 3.0 | – | 225 |
| Starter & Quick Starter | A1 | YLE Movers | 1.0–2.0 | – | – |

You can find details and a full list of books and teachers' resources on our website:
www.oup.com/elt/gradedreaders